THE USBORNE INTERNET-LINKED

FIRST THOUSAND WORDS

IN ITALIAN

With Internet-linked pronunciation guide

Heather Amery

Illustrated by Stephen Cartwright

Edited by Nicole Irving, Mairi Mackinnon and Katie Daynes

Design... ...h Ahmed

Ita... ...anaco

With thanks to Terry Shannon

About Usborne Quicklinks

To access the Usborne Quicklinks Web site for this book, go to
www.usborne-quicklinks.com
and enter the keywords "1000 italian". There you can:

● listen to the first thousand words in Italian, read by a native Italian speaker

● print out some Italian picture puzzles for free

● find links to other useful Web sites about Italy and the Italian language

Listening to the words

To hear the words in this book, you will need your Web browser
(e.g. Internet Explorer or Netscape Navigator) and a programme that lets you play sound
(such as RealPlayer® or Windows® Media Player). These programmes are free and, if you
don't already have one of them, you can download them from Usborne Quicklinks.
Your computer also needs a sound card but most
computers already have one of these.

Note for parents and guardians

Please ensure that your children read and follow the Internet safety
guidelines displayed on the Usborne Quicklinks Web site.

The links in Usborne Quicklinks are regularly reviewed and updated.
However, the content of a Web site may change at any time and Usborne Publishing
is not responsible for the content on any Web site other than its own. We recommend
that children are supervised while on the Internet, that they do not use
Internet Chat Rooms, and that you use Internet filtering software to block
unsuitable material. For more information, see the **Net Help**
area on the Usborne Quicklinks Web site.

On every double page with pictures,
there is a little yellow duck to look for.
Can you find it?

About this book

This is a great book for anyone starting to learn Italian. You'll find it easy to learn new words by looking at the small, labelled pictures. Then you can practise the words by talking about the large central pictures. This book also has its own Usborne Quicklinks Web site where you can listen to all the Italian words, print out Italian picture puzzles, and follow links to some other fun and useful Web sites.

Masculine and feminine words

When you look at Italian words for things such as "chair" or "man", you will see that they have **il**, **lo**, **la** or **l'** in front of them. This is because all Italian words for things and people are either masculine or feminine. **Il** or **lo** are the words for "the" in front of a masculine word and **la** is "the" in front of a feminine word. You use **l'** in front of words that begin with "a", "e", "i", "o" or "u". In front of the words that are plural (more than one, such as "chairs" or "men"), the Italian word for "the" is **i** or **gli** for masculine words, and **le** for feminine words.

All the labels in this book show words for things with **il**, **lo**, **la**, **l'**, **i**, **gli** or **le**. Always learn them with this little word.

Looking at Italian words

A few Italian words have an accent on the last letter of the word. This is a sign written over the letter, and means that the last part of the word is stressed when it is spoken.

Saying Italian words

The best way to learn how to say Italian words is to listen to an Italian speaker and repeat what you hear. You can listen to all the words in this book on the Usborne Quicklinks Web site. For more information on how to do this, see the page on the left. At the back of this book, there is also a word list with an easy pronunciation guide for each Italian word.

A computer is not essential

If you don't have access to the Internet, don't worry. This book is a complete and excellent Italian word book on its own.

A casa

la vasca

il sapone

il rubinetto

la carta igienica

lo spazzolino

l'acqua

il water

la spugna

il lavandino

la doccia

il letto

Il bagno

Il soggiorno

l'asciugamano

il dentifricio

la radio

il cuscino

il Compact Disc

la moquette

il divano

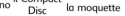

4

la sedia

il piumone

il pettine

il lenzuolo

il tappeto

l'armadio

La camera da letto

il guanciale

il cassettone

lo specchio

la spazzola

la lampada

L'ingresso

i poster

l'attaccapanni

il telefono

le scale

radiatore

la videocassetta

il giornale

il tavolino

le lettere

5

La cucina

il frigorifero

i bicchieri

l'orologio

lo sgabello

i cucchiaini

l'interruttore

il detersivo

la chiave

la porta

il lavello

l'aspirapolvere

le pentole

le forchette

il grembiule

l'asse da stiro

la spazzatura

6

il bollitore

i coltelli

 lo spazzolone

lo straccio

le mattonelle

la scopa

 la lavatrice

 la paletta

 il cassetto

 i piattini

 la padella

 la cucina

 i mestoli

 i piatti

 il ferro da stiro

 l'armadietto

l'asciugatoio

le tazze

i fiammiferi

 la spazzola

 le scodelle

7

Il giardino

la carriola

l'alveare

la chiocciola

i mattoni

il piccione

la vanga

la coccinella

la pattumiera

i semi

il casotto

l'annaffiatoio

il verme

i fiori

l'annaffiatore

la zappa

la vespa

8

l'ape

la paletta

l'osso

la siepe

il forcone

il tosaerba

il sentiero

le foglie

l'albero

il fumo

il bruco

il rastrello

il nido

i ramoscelli

l'erba

la carrozzina

la scala

il falò

il tubo di gomma

la serra

la morsa

la carta vetrata

il trapano

la scala

la sega

la segatura

il calendario

Il laboratorio

le viti

la cassetta degli arnesi

il cacciavite

l'asse

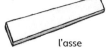
i trucioli

il temperino

le bullette

il ragno

i bulloni

i dadi

la ragnatela

la botte

la mosca

l'ascia

il metro

il martello

la lima

la vernice

il legno

i chiodi

il piano di lavoro

i barattoli

la pialla

11

La strada

il negozio

il buco

il bar

l'ambulanza

il marciapiede

l'antenna

il comignolo

il tetto

la scavatrice

l'albergo

l'autobus

l'uomo

la macchina
della polizia

le condutture

il martello
pneumatico

la scuola

il campo giochi

il taxi
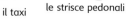 le strisce pedonali
 la fabbrica
 il camion
il semaforo
 il cinema

 il furgone

 lo schiacciasassi

 il rimorchio

 la casa

 il mercato

 gli scalini

 la motocicletta

 il palazzo

 la bicicletta
l'autopompa
il vigile urbano
la macchina la donna
il lampione

13

I giocattoli

il trenino

i dadi

il flauto dolce

il robot

il robot

i tamburi

la collana

la macchina
fotografica

le perline

le bambole

la chitarra

l'anello

l'armonica

la casa
delle bambole

il
fischietto

le
costruzioni

il castello

il sottomarino

la tromba

le frecce

l'arco

il paracadute

la barca

i colori per il viso

lo schiacciasassi

le maschere

la macchina da corsa

il cavallo a dondolo

il salvadanaio

le biglie

le marionette

il pianoforte

gli astronauti

la gru

la plastilina

il fucile

i soldatini

gli acquarelli

il razzo

15

le altalene

Il parco

la panchina

la buca di sabbia

il picnic

l'aquilone

il gelato

il cane

il cancello

il sentiero

la rana

lo scivolo

i girini

il lago

i rollerblades

il cespuglio

16

il bebè

 lo skateboard

 la terra

il passeggino

 l'altalena a bilico

 i bambini

 il triciclo

 gli uccelli

 la cancellata

 la palla

 la barca

 lo spago

 la pozzanghera

 gli anatroccoli

 la corda per saltare

 l'aiuola

i cigni

il guinzaglio

 le anatre

 gli alberi

17

Lo zoo

le ali

l'aquila

l'ippopotamo

il panda

le zampe

il gorilla

il canguro

il pipistrello

la scimmia

l'iceberg

la coda

il pinguino

il lupo

il coccodrillo

l'orso

le piume

il pellicano

il delfino

lo struzzo

il leone

i leoncini

la giraffa

18

le corna

il cervo

il dromedario

la foca

l'orso polare

la tartaruga

la proboscide

il rinoceronte

l'elefante

il bisonte

il castoro

la zebra

il serpente

la capra

lo squalo

la balena

la tigre

il leopardo

19

i binari

I trasporti

l'elicottero

il locomotore

i respingenti

i vagoni

il macchinista

il treno merci

la pensilina

La stazione ferroviaria

La stazione di servizio

il controllore

la valigia

la biglietteria
automatica

i segnali

lo zaino

i fari

il motore

la ruota

la batteria

20

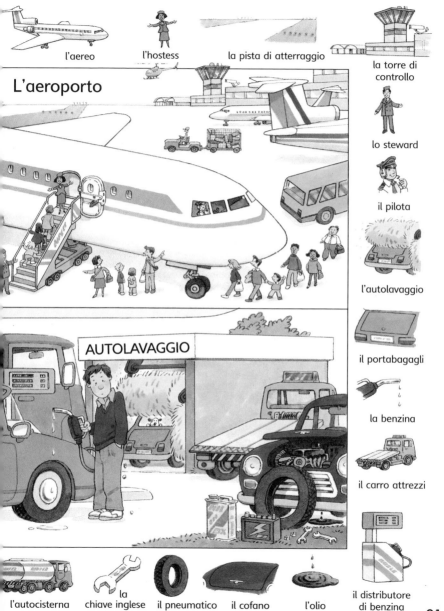

l'aereo

l'hostess

la pista di atterraggio

la torre di controllo

lo steward

il pilota

l'autolavaggio

il portabagagli

la benzina

il carro attrezzi

L'aeroporto

AUTOLAVAGGIO

l'autocisterna

la chiave inglese

il pneumatico

il cofano

l'olio

il distributore di benzina

21

il mulino a vento

La campagna

la montagna

la mongolfiera

la farfalla

la lucertola

le pietre

la volpe

il ruscello

il cartello stradale

il riccio

la chiusa

lo scoiattolo

la foresta

il tasso

il fiume

la strada

le tende

il canale

i ceppi

il villaggio

la falena

il ponte

la chiatta

la cascata

il gufo

la galleria

i volpacchiotti

la talpa

il pescatore

i massi

il rospo

il treno

la roulotte

la collina

23

il mucchio di fieno

La fattoria

il gallo

il cane pastore

le anatre

gli agnelli

lo stagno

i pulcini

il fienile

il porcile

il toro

gli anatroccoli

il pollaio

il trattore

le oche

l'autocisterna

il capannone

il fango

il carretto

24

l'agricoltore

il campo

le galline

il vitello

la staccionata

la sella

la stalla

la mucca

l'aratro

il frutteto

la scuderia

i maialini

la pastorella

i tacchini

lo spaventapasseri

il fieno

le pecore

le balle di paglia

il cavallo

i maiali

la casa colonica

25

la barca a vela

Al mare

la conchiglia

il mare

il remo

il faro

la paletta

il secchiello

la stella marina

il castello
di sabbia

l'ombrellone

la bandiera

il marinaio

il granchio

il gabbiano

l'isola

il motoscafo

lo sci nautico

le onde

il cappello da sole

la scogliera

la nave

la canoa

la fune

i ciottoli

le alghe

la rete

la pagaia

il peschereccio

le pinne

l'asino

il pesce

il costume da bagno

la petroliera

la spiaggia

la barca a remi

la sedia a sdraio

27

A scuola

le forbici

le addizioni

la gomma

il righello

le fotografie

i pennarelli

le puntine
da disegno

i colori

il bambino

la matita

la lavagna

il banco

i libri

la penna

la colla

i gessetti

il disegno

28

il cestino della carta

l'insegnante

la scatola

la carta geografica

il pennello

il soffitto

la parete

il pavimento

il quaderno

l'alfabeto

la spilla

l'acquario

la carta

l'avvolgibile

il cavalletto

la maniglia della porta

la pianta

il mappamondo

la bambina

i pastelli

la lampada

29

L'ospedale

l'infermiere

il cotone idrofilo

la medicina

l'ascensore

la vestaglia

le grucce

le pillole

il vassoio

l'orologio

il termometro

la tenda

l'orsacchiotto

la mela

il gesso

la fascia

la sedia a rotelle

il puzzle

la dottoressa

la siringa

30

Dal dottore

le pantofole

il computer

il cerotto

la banana

l'uva

il cestino

i giocattoli

la pera

le cartoline

il pannolino

il bastone

il televisore

la camicia
da notte

il pigiama

l'arancia

i fazzoletti
di carta

il fumetto

la sala d'aspetto

31

La festa

il palloncino

la cioccolata

la caramella

la finestra

i fuochi d'artificio

il nastro

la torta

i regali

la cannuccia la candela le decorazioni di carta

i giocattoli

il mandarino

il salame

 la musicassetta

la salsiccia

 le patatine

 i costumi

 la ciliegia

 il succo di frutta

 il lampone

 la fragola

 la lampadina

 il panino

il burro

il biscotto

il formaggio

il pane

 la tovaglia

33

Il negozio

il pompelmo

la carota

il cavolfiore

il porro

il fungo

il cetriolo

il limone

il sedano

l'albicocca

il melone

la borsa della spesa

FORMAGGI

FRUTTA E VERDURA

la cipolla   il cavolo   la pesca   la lattuga   i piselli   il pomodoro

le uova

la susina

la farina

la bilancia

i barattoli

la carne

l'ananas

lo yogurt

il cestino

le bottiglie

la borsa

il borsellino

i soldi

il cibo in scatola

le patate

gli spinaci

i fagiolini

la cassa

la zucca

il carrello

I pasti

la colazione

il pranzo

l'uovo sodo

il caffè

l'uovo fritto

il pane tostato

la marmellata

la panna

il latte

i cereali

la cioccolata calda

lo zucchero

il miele

il sale

il pepe

il tè

la teiera

le frittelle

i panini

la cena

il prosciutto

la minestra

la frittata

le bacchette

l'insalata

l'hamburger

il pollo

il riso

il ketchup

gli spaghetti

il purè

la pizza

le patatine fritte

i dolci

Me stesso

la testa

i capelli

il viso

 le sopracciglia

 l'occhio

 il naso

  la guancia

 la bocca

 le labbra

 i denti

  la lingua

 il mento

il braccio

il gomito

la pancia

le orecchie

il collo

le spalle

le dita dei piedi

il piede

la gamba

il ginocchio

il torace

la schiena

il sedere

la mano

il pollice

le dita della mano

I vestiti

 i calzini

 le mutande

 la canottiera

 i pantaloni

 i jeans

 la maglietta

 la gonna

 la camicia

 la cravatta

 i pantaloncini

 la calzamaglia

 il vestito

 il maglione

 la felpa

 il cardigan

 la sciarpa

 il fazzoletto

 le scarpe da ginnastica

 le scarpe

 i sandali

 gli stivali di gomma

 i guanti

 la cintura

 la fibbia

 la cerniera lampo

 i lacci per le scarpe

 i bottoni

 le asole

le tasche

 il cappotto

 il giubbotto

 il berretto

 il cappello

I mestieri

l'attore   l'attrice

il cuoco

i ballerini

i cantanti

l'astronauta

il macellaio

i poliziotti

il falegname

il pompiere

l'artista

il giudice

i meccanici

40

il parrucchiere

la camionista

il conducente di autobus

il cameriere   la cameriera

il postino

la dentista

l'imbianchino

il subacqueo

la fornaia

La famiglia

la zia   lo zio

il nonno

il figlio   la figlia   la madre   il padre
il fratello la sorella la moglie   il marito

il cugino   la nonna

41

Le azioni

ridere

sorridere

piangere

pensare

ascoltare

acchiappare

lanciare

rompere

dipingere

scrivere

spaccare

tagliare

mangiare

parlare

scavare

bere

fare

saltare

portare

camminare a carponi

ballare

lavarsi

lavorare a maglia

giocare

guardare

arrampicarsi

prendere

saltare la corda

fare a botte

dormire

cucire

aspettare

cucinare

nascondersi

comprare

leggere

cantare

soffiare

spingere

spazzare

raccogliere

tirare

cadere

camminare

correre

stare seduti

43

I contrari

lontano

vicino

buono

cattivo

in cima

in fondo

freddo   caldo

bagnato   asciutto

sopra

sotto

sporco   pulito

grasso   magro

aperto   chiuso

piccolo   grande

pochi   molti

primo   ultimo

sinistra

fuori

dentro

facile

difficile

vuoto

pieno

morbido

duro

davanti

alto

lento

veloce

dietro

basso

lungo

corto

morto

vivo

scuro

chiaro

vecchio

su

destra

nuovo

giù

45

I giorni

domenica

giovedì

martedì

mercoledì

lunedì

venerdì

sabato

il calendario

la mattina

la sera

il sole

la notte

la luna

la stella

lo Spazio

il pianeta

l'astronave

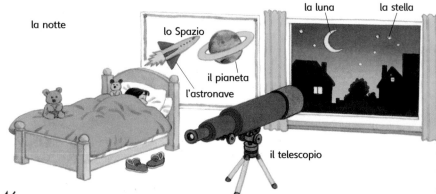

il telescopio

Giorni speciali

il compleanno

il biglietto
di auguri

le candeline

la vacanza

il regalo

la torta

il matrimonio

la macchina
fotografica

la damigella
d'onore

la sposa

lo sposo

il fotografo

Natale

la renna

la slitta

Babbo Natale

l'albero di Natale

47

Il tempo

l'ombrello

la pioggia

il lampo

la nebbia

il sole

le nuvole

il cielo

la neve

la rugiada

il vento

la foschia

la brina

l'arcobaleno

Le stagioni

la primavera

l'estate

l'autunno

l'inverno

Gli animali domestici

il criceto

il veterinario

il porcellino d'India

la cuccia

il cagnolino

il cane

il pappagallino

il pappagallo

il becco

il cibo

il coniglio

il canarino

la gabbia

il gatto   la cesta

il topolino

il gattino

il latte

i pesci rossi

49

Lo sport

il canottaggio

lo snowboard

la vela

il windsurf

la pallacanestro

la racchetta

il cricket

il karatè

la mazza

il tennis

il football americano

la ginnastica artistica

la palla

la pesca

la canna da pesca

l'esca

la danza

il baseball

il rugby

i tuffi

la piscina

il nuoto

la corsa campestre

il tiro con l'arco

il bersaglio

il volo libero

il casco

il jogging

il ciclismo

l'alpinismo

il judo

il cavallo

il pony

l'armadietto

lo spogliatoio

l'equitazione

il badminton

il calcio

i pattini

il ping-pong

il pattinaggio su ghiaccio

i bastoncini da sci

la seggiovia

gli sci

lo sci

il sumo

51

I colori

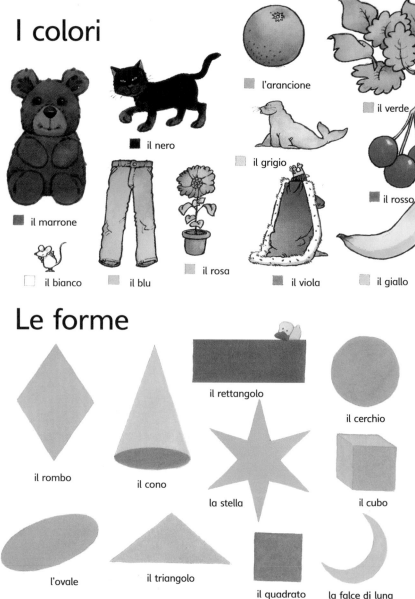

l'arancione

il verde

il nero

il grigio

il rosso

il marrone

il bianco

il blu

il rosa

il viola

il giallo

Le forme

il rettangolo

il cerchio

il rombo

il cono

la stella

il cubo

l'ovale

il triangolo

il quadrato

la falce di luna

I numeri

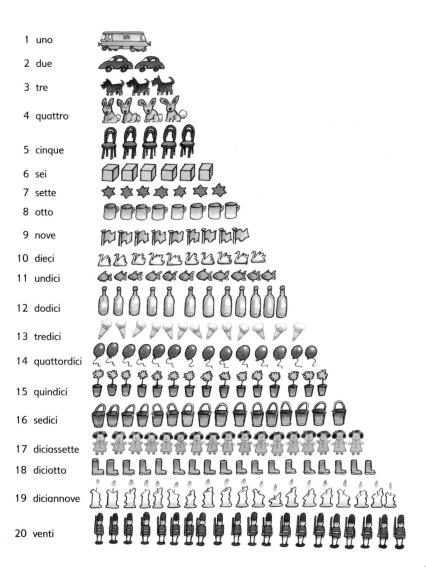

1 uno

2 due

3 tre

4 quattro

5 cinque

6 sei

7 sette

8 otto

9 nove

10 dieci

11 undici

12 dodici

13 tredici

14 quattordici

15 quindici

16 sedici

17 diciassette

18 diciotto

19 diciannove

20 venti

Il luna park

la giostra

il tappetino

lo scivolo

la ruota

il trenino dei fantasmi

il pop-corn

il tiro al cerchietto

le montagne russe

il tiro a segno

l'autoscontro

lo zucchero filato

54

Il circo

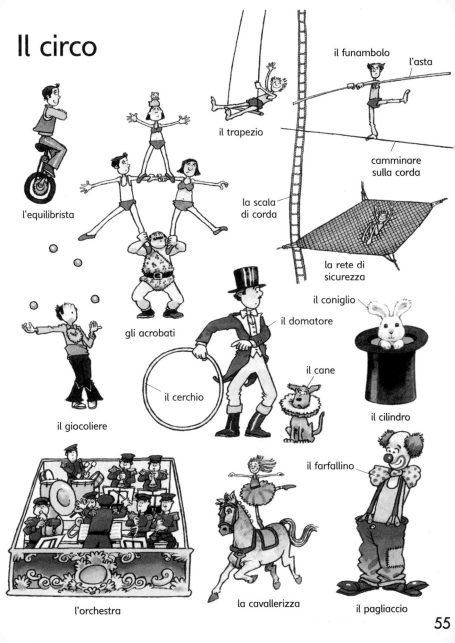

l'equilibrista

il trapezio

il funambolo

l'asta

camminare sulla corda

la scala di corda

la rete di sicurezza

gli acrobati

il giocoliere

il cerchio

il domatore

il coniglio

il cane

il cilindro

l'orchestra

la cavallerizza

il farfallino

il pagliaccio

55

Word list

In this list you can find all the Italian words in this book. They are listed in alphabetical order. Next to each one, you can see its pronunciation (how to say it) in letters *like this*, and then its English translation.

Remember that Italian nouns (words for things) are either masculine or feminine (see page 3). In the list, each one has **il**, **lo**, **la**, **l'**, **i**, **gli** or **le** in front of it. These all mean "the". The words with **il** or **lo** are masculine, those with **la** are feminine. Italian nouns that begin with "a", "e", "i", "o" or "u" have **l'** in front of them. After the word you will see **(m)** or **(f)** to show whether it is masculine or feminine.

Plural nouns (a noun is plural if you are talking about more than one, for example "cats") have **i** or **gli** in front if they are masculine, or **le** if they are feminine.

About Italian pronunciation
Read the pronunciation as if it were an English word, but try to remember the following points about how Italian words are said:

All the letters in an Italian word are sounded, except 'h'; Double letters, like 'll' or 'nn', sound a little longer than usual;

c before *e* or *i* is pronounced *ch*;

ch before *e* or *i* is pronounced *k*;

gh before *e* or *i* is pronounced *g* as in *get*;

sc before *e* or *i* is pronounced *sh*;

z is pronounced *ts*.

Most Italian words have a part that you stress, or say louder (like the "day" part of the English word "today"). So you know which part of each word you should stress, it is shown in letters *like this* in the pronunciation guide;

In the guide, *ay* is like the *a* in date;

o is like the *o* in *hot*;

ow is like the *ow* in *cow*;

g is always like the *g* in *get*;

ly is like the *lli* in *million*;

ny is like the *ni* in *onion*;

ye is always like the *ye* in *yet*.

A

acchiappare	*akkyapparay*	to catch
l'acqua (f)	*lakwa*	water
gli acquarelli	*lyee akwarellee*	paints
l'acquario (m)	*lakwaryo*	aquarium
gli acrobati	*lyee akrobatee*	acrobats
le addizioni	*lay addeetsyonee*	sums
l'aereo (m)	*la-ayrayo*	aeroplane
l'aeroporto (m)	*la-ayroporto*	airport
gli agnelli	*lyee anyellee*	lambs
l'agricoltore	*lagreekoltoray*	farmer
l'aiuola (f)	*la-yuola*	flower bed
l'albergo (m)	*lalbairgo*	hotel
gli alberi	*lyee albairee*	trees
l'albero (m)	*lalbairo*	tree
l'albero (m) di Natale	*lalbairo dee natalay*	Christmas tree
l'albicocca (f)	*lalbeekokka*	apricot
l'alfabeto (m)	*lalfabayto*	alphabet
le alghe	*lay algay*	seaweed
le ali	*lay alee*	wings
l'alpinismo (m)	*lalpeeneezmo*	climbing
l'altalena (f) a bilico	*laltalayna a beeleeko*	seesaw
le altalene	*lay altalaynay*	swings
alto	*alto*	high
l'alveare (m)	*lalvayaray*	beehive
l'ambulanza (f)	*lamboolantsa*	ambulance
l'ananas (m)	*lananass*	pineapple
le anatre	*lay anatray*	ducks
gli anatroccoli	*lyee anatrokkolee*	ducklings
l'anello (m)	*lanello*	ring
gli animali domestici	*lyee aneemalee domesteechee*	pets
l'annaffiatoio (m)	*lanaffyatoyo*	watering can
l'annaffiatore (m)	*lanaffyatoray*	sprinkler
l'antenna (f)	*lantenna*	aerial
l'ape (f)	*lapay*	bee

aperto	*apairto*	open
l'aquila (f)	*lakweela*	eagle
l'aquilone (m)	*lakweelonay*	kite
l'arancia (f)	*larancha*	orange (fruit)
l'arancione (m)	*aranchonay*	orange (colour)
l'aratro (m)	*laratro*	plough
l'arco (m)	*larko*	bow (and arrows)
l'arcobaleno (m)	*larkobalayno*	rainbow
l'armadietto (m)	*larmadyetto*	cupboard
l'armadio (m)	*larmadyo*	wardrobe
l'armonica (f)	*larmoneeka*	mouth organ
arrampicarsi	*arrampeekarsee*	to climb
l'artista (m/f)	*larteesta*	artist
l'ascensore (m)	*lashensoray*	lift
l'ascia (f)	*lasha*	axe
l'asciugamano (m)	*lashoogamano*	towel
l'asciugatoio (m)	*lashoogatoyo*	tea towel
asciutto	*ashootto*	dry
ascoltare	*askoltaray*	to listen
l'asino (m)	*lazeeno*	donkey
le asole	*lay azolay*	button holes
aspettare	*aspettaray*	to wait
l'aspirapolvere (m)	*laspeerapolvairay*	vacuum cleaner
l'asse (f)	*lassay*	plank
l'asse (f) da stiro	*lassay da steero*	ironing board
l'asta (f)	*lasta*	pole
l'astronave (f)	*lastronavay*	spaceship
l'astronauta (m)	*lastronowta*	astronaut
gli astronauti	*lyee astronowtee*	astronauts, spacemen
l'attaccapanni (m)	*lattakkapannee*	pegs
l'attore (m)	*lattoray*	actor
l'attrice (f)	*lattreechay*	actress
l'autobus (m)	*lowtoboos*	bus
l'autocisterna (f)	*lowtocheestairna*	tanker lorry
l'autolavaggio (m)	*lowtolavajjo*	car wash
l'autopompa (f)	*lowtopompa*	fire engine

56

l'autoscontro (m)	lowto**skon**tro	dodgems
l'autunno (m)	low**toon**no	autumn
l'avvolgibile (m)	lavvol**jee**beelay	blind
le azioni	lay at**syo**nee	actions

B

Babbo Natale	**babbo** na**ta**lay	Father Christmas
le bacchette	lay bak**ket**tay	chopsticks
il badminton	eel **bad**meenton	badminton
bagnato	ban**ya**to	wet
il bagno	eel **ban**yo	bathroom
la balena	la ba**lay**na	whale
ballare	bal**la**ray	to dance
le balle di paglia	lay **ball**ay dee **pal**ya	straw bales
i ballerini	ee bal**lair**eenee	dancers
la bambina	la bam**bee**na	girl
i bambini	ee bam**bee**nee	children
il bambino	eel bam**bee**no	boy
le bambole	lay **bam**bolay	dolls
la banana	la ba**na**na	banana
il banco	eel **ban**ko	desk
la bandiera	la band**yai**ra	flag
il bar	eel bar	café
i barattoli	ee ba**rat**tolee	pots, jars
la barca	la **bar**ka	boat
la barca a vela	la **bar**ka a **vay**la	sailing boat
la barca a remi	la **bar**ka a **ray**mee	rowing boat
il baseball	eel bay**zbol**	baseball
basso	**bas**so	low
il bastone	eel bas**to**nay	stick
i bastoncini da sci	ee baston**chee**nee da shee	ski poles
la batteria	la bat**tair**eea	battery
il bebè	eel be**bay**	baby
il becco	eel **bek**ko	beak
la benzina	la bent**see**na	petrol
bere	**bair**ay	to drink
il berretto	eel bair**ret**to	cap
il bersaglio	eel bair**sal**yo	target
il bianco	eel **byan**ko	white
i bicchieri	ee beek**kyair**ee	glasses (for drinking)
la bicicletta	la beechee**klet**ta	bicycle
le biglie	lay **beel**yay	marbles
la biglietteria automatica	la beelyet**tair**eea owt**oma**teeka	ticket machine
il biglietto di auguri	eel beel**yet**to dee ow**goo**ree	birthday card
la bilancia	la bee**lan**cha	scales
i binari	ee bee**na**ree	railway track
il biscotto	eel bees**kot**to	biscuit
il bisonte	eel bee**zon**tay	bison
il blu	eel bloo	blue
la bocca	la **bok**ka	mouth
il bollitore	eel bollee**to**ray	kettle
la borsa	la **bor**sa	handbag
la borsa della spesa	la **bor**sa **del**la **spay**za	carrier bag
il borsellino	eel borsel**lee**no	wallet
la botte	la **bot**tay	barrel
le bottiglie	lay bot**teel**yay	bottles
i bottoni	ee bot**to**nee	buttons
il braccio	eel **bra**cho	arm
la brina	la **bree**na	frost
il bruco	eel **broo**ko	caterpillar

la buca di sabbia	la **boo**ka dee **sab**bya	sandpit
il buco	eel **boo**ko	hole
le bullette	lay **bool**etay	tacks
i bulloni	ee bool**lo**nee	bolts
buono	**bwo**no	good
il burro	eel **boor**ro	butter

C

il cacciavite	eel kacha**vee**tay	screwdriver
cadere	ka**dai**ray	to fall
il caffè	eel ka**ffay**	coffee
il cagnolino	eel kanyo**lee**no	puppy
il calcio	eel **kal**cho	football
caldo	**kal**do	hot
il calendario	eel kalen**dar**yo	calendar
la calzamaglia	la kaltsa**mal**ya	tights
i calzini	ee kalt**see**nee	socks
la camera da letto	la **kam**aira da **let**to	bedroom
la cameriera	la kamair**yai**ra	waitress
il cameriere	eel kamair**yai**ray	waiter
la camicia	la ka**mee**cha	shirt
la camicia da notte	la ka**mee**cha da **not**tay	nightdress
il camion	eel **kam**yon	lorry
il/la camionista	la kamyo**nees**ta	lorry driver
camminare	kamm**een**aray	to walk
camminare a carponi	kamm**een**aray a kar**po**nee	to crawl
camminare sulla corda	kamm**een**aray **sool**la **kor**da	to walk a tightrope
la campagna	la kam**pan**ya	country
il campo	eel **kam**po	field
il campo giochi	eel **kam**po **jok**ee	playground
il canale	eel ka**nal**ay	canal
il canarino	eel kana**ree**no	canary
la cancellata	la kanchel**la**ta	railings
il cancello	eel kan**chel**lo	gate
la candela	la kan**day**la	candle
le candeline	lay kande**lee**nay	cake candles
il cane	eel **kan**ay	dog
il cane pastore	eel **kan**ay pas**to**ray	sheepdog
il canguro	eel kan**goo**ro	kangaroo
la canna da pesca	la **kan**na da **pes**ka	fishing rod
la cannuccia	la kan**noo**cha	straw
la canoa	la kan**o**a	canoe
il canottaggio	eel kan**ot**tajjo	rowing
la canottiera	la kanott**yai**ra	vest
i cantanti	ee kan**tan**tee	singers
cantare	kan**ta**ray	to sing
il capannone	eel kapan**no**nay	barn
i capelli	ee ka**pel**lee	hair
il cappello	eel kap**pel**lo	hat
il cappello da sole	eel kap**pel**lo da **so**lay	sun hat
il cappotto	eel kap**pot**to	coat
la capra	la **kap**ra	goat
la caramella	la kara**mel**la	sweet
il cardigan	eel **kar**deegan	cardigan
la carne	la **kar**nay	meat
la carota	la ka**ro**ta	carrot
il carrello	eel kar**rel**lo	trolley
il carretto	eel kar**ret**to	cart
la carriola	la kar**ryo**la	wheelbarrow
il carro attrezzi	eel **kar**ro at**tret**tsee	breakdown lorry
la carrozzina	la karrott**see**na	pram
la carta	la **kar**ta	paper

la carta geografica	la **karta** jayo**gra**feeka	map
la carta igienica	la **karta** ee**je**neeka	toilet paper
la carta vetrata	la **karta** ve**tra**ta	sandpaper
il cartello stradale	eel kar**tello** stra**da**lay	signpost
le cartoline	lay karto**lee**nay	cards
la casa	la **ka**za	house
la casa colonica	la **ka**za kolo**nee**ka	farmhouse
la casa delle bambole	la **ka**za **del**lay **bam**bolay	dolls' house
la cascata	la kas**ka**ta	waterfall
il casco	eel **kas**ko	helmet
il casotto	eel ka**zotto**	shed
la cassa	la **kas**sa	checkout
la cassetta degli arnesi	la kas**setta del**yee **ar**naysee	tool box
il cassetto	eel kas**setto**	drawer
il cassettone	eel kas**setto**nay	chest of drawers
il castello	eel kas**tello**	castle
il castello di sabbia	eel kas**tello** dee **sabb**ya	sandcastle
il castoro	eel kas**toro**	beaver
cattivo	kat**tee**vo	bad
la cavallerizza	la kavallai**reetts**a	bareback rider
il cavalletto	eel kaval**letto**	easel
il cavallo	eel ka**vallo**	horse
il cavallo a dondolo	eel ka**vallo** a **dondolo**	rocking horse
il cavolfiore	eel kavol**fyoray**	cauliflower
il cavolo	eel **ka**volo	cabbage
la cena	la **chay**na	supper, dinner
i ceppi	ee **chep**pee	logs
il cerchio	eel **chair**kyo	circle, hoop
i cereali	ee chairay**alee**	cereal
la cerniera lampo	la chairn**yai**ra **lam**po	zip
il cerotto	eel chai**rotto**	sticking plaster
il cervo	eel **chair**vo	deer
il cespuglio	eel ches**pool**yo	bush
la cesta	la **ches**ta	basket
il cestino	eel ches**tee**no	shopping basket
il cestino della carta	eel ches**tee**no **della karta**	waste paper basket
il cetriolo	eel chetree**olo**	cucumber
chiaro	**kya**ro	light
la chiatta	la **kya**tta	barge
la chiave	la **kya**vay	key
la chiave inglese	la **kya**vay eeng**lay**zay	spanner
la chiocciola	la **kyo**chola	snail
i chiodi	ee **kyo**dee	nails
la chitarra	la kee**tarr**a	guitar
la chiusa	la **kyoo**za	lock (canal)
chiuso	**kyoo**zo	closed
il cibo in scatola	eel **chee**bo een s**katola**	tinned food
il cibo	eel **chee**bo	food
il ciclismo	eel chee**kleez**mo	cycling
il cielo	eel **chay**lo	sky
i cigni	ee **chee**nyee	swans
la ciliegia	la chee**lye**ja	cherry
il cilindro	eel chee**leen**dro	top hat
il cinema	eel **chee**nayma	cinema
cinque	**cheen**quay	five
la cintura	la cheen**too**ra	belt
la cioccolata	la chokko**la**ta	chocolate
la cioccolata calda	la chokko**la**ta **kal**da	hot chocolate
i ciottoli	ee **chott**olee	pebbles
la cipolla	la chee**poll**a	onion
il circo	eel **cheer**ko	circus
la coccinella	la kochee**nella**	ladybird
il coccodrillo	eel kokko**dreello**	crocodile
la coda	la **ko**da	tail
il cofano	eel **ko**fano	bonnet
la colazione	la kola**tsyo**nay	breakfast
la colla	la **koll**a	glue
la collana	la kol**la**na	necklace
la collina	la kol**lee**na	hill
il collo	eel **kollo**	neck
i colori	ee ko**lo**ree	colours, paints
i colori per il viso	ee ko**lo**ree pair eel **vee**zo	face paints
i coltelli	ee kol**tellee**	knives
il comignolo	eel komee**nyolo**	chimney
il Compact Disc	eel **kom**pat deesk	CD
il compleanno	eel komplea**nno**	birthday
comprare	kom**pra**ray	to buy
il computer	eel kom**pyoo**tair	computer
la conchiglia	la kon**keel**ya	shell
il conducente di autobus	eel kondoo**chen**tay dee **ow**toboos	bus driver
le condutture	lay kondoo**too**ray	pipes
il coniglio	eel ko**neel**yo	rabbit
il cono	eel **ko**no	cone
i contrari	ee kon**tra**ree	opposites
il controllore	eel kontrol**lo**ray	ticket inspector
la corda per saltare	la **kor**da pair sal**ta**ray	skipping rope
le corna	lay **kor**na	horns
correre	**kor**rairay	to run
la corsa campestre	la **kor**sa kam**pes**tray	running race
corto	**kor**to	short
le costruzioni	lay kostroo**tsyo**nee	building blocks
il costume da bagno	eel kos**too**may da **ba**nyo	swimsuit
i costumi	ee kos**too**mee	fancy dress
il cotone idrofilo	eel **ko**tonay eed**ro**feelo	cotton wool
la cravatta	la kra**vatta**	tie
il criceto	eel kree**chay**to	hamster
il cricket	eel **kree**ket	cricket
il cubo	eel **koo**bo	cube
i cucchiaini	ee kookkya-**ee**nee	teaspoons
la cuccia	la **koo**cha	kennel
la cucina	la koo**chee**na	kitchen
cucinare	koochee**na**ray	to cook
cucire	koo**chee**ray	to sew
il cugino	eel koo**jee**no	cousin
il cuoco	eel **kwo**ko	cook
il cuscino	eel koo**shee**no	cushion

D

i dadi (da officina)	ee **da**dee (da offee**chee**na)	nuts (workshop)
i dadi (per giocare)	ee **da**dee (pair jo**ka**ray)	dice
la damigella d'onore	la damee**jella** do**no**ray	bridesmaid
la danza	la **dan**tsa	dancing
davanti	da**van**tee	front
le decorazioni di carta	lay dekora**tsyo**nee dee **karta**	paper chains
il delfino	eel del**fee**no	dolphin
i denti	ee **den**tee	teeth
il dentifricio	eel dentee**free**cho	toothpaste
il/la dentista	eel/la den**tee**sta	dentist
dentro	**den**tro	inside
destra	**des**tra	right
il detersivo	eel detair**see**vo	washing powder
diciannove	deechan**no**vay	nineteen
diciassette	deechas**sett**ay	seventeen
diciotto	dee**chotto**	eighteen
dieci	**dye**chee	ten
dietro	**dye**tro	behind
difficile	deef**fee**cheelay	difficult
dipingere	dee**peen**jairay	to paint

58

il disegno	eel dee**senyo**	drawing
il distributore di benzina	eel dee**stree**boo**toray** dee bent**seena**	petrol pump
le dita dei piedi	lay **deeta** day **pye**dee	toes
le dita della mano	lay **deeta della mano**	fingers
il divano	eel dee**vano**	sofa
la doccia	la **docha**	shower
dodici	**dodeechee**	twelve
i dolci	ee **dolchee**	pudding
il domatore	eel doma**toray**	ringmaster
domenica	dome**neeka**	Sunday
la donna	la **donna**	woman
dormire	dor**meeray**	to sleep
il dottore	eel dot**toray**	doctor
la dottoressa	la dotto**ressa**	(woman) doctor
il dromedario	eel drome**daryo**	camel
due	**doo**ay	two
duro	**doo**ro	hard

E

l'elefante (m)	lele**fantay**	elephant
l'elicottero (m)	leleko**ttairo**	helicopter
l'equilibrista (m)	lekweelee**breesta**	unicyclist
l'equitazione (f)	lekweeta**tsyonay**	riding
l'erba (f)	**lairba**	grass
l'esca (f)	**les**ka	bait
l'estate (m)	le**statay**	summer

F

la fabbrica	la **fabb**reeka	factory
facile	**fa**cheelay	easy
i fagiolini	ee fajo**lee**nee	beans
la falce di luna	la **fal**chay dee **loo**na	crescent
il falegname	eel falen**yamay**	carpenter
la falena	la fa**layna**	moth
il falò	eel fa**lo**	bonfire
la famiglia	la fa**meelya**	family
il fango	eel **fango**	mud
fare	**fa**ray	to make, to do
fare a botte	**fa**ray a **bott**ay	to fight
la farfalla	la far**falla**	butterfly
il farfallino	eel farfa**lleeno**	bow tie
la farina	la fa**reena**	flour
il faro	eel **faro**	lighthouse
la fascia	la **fasha**	bandage
la fattoria	la fatto**reea**	farm
i fazzoletti di carta	ee fattso**lett**ee dee **karta**	tissues
il fazzoletto	eel fattso**letto**	handkerchief
la felpa	la **felpa**	sweatshirt
il ferro da stiro	eel **fair**ro da **steero**	iron
la festa	la **festa**	party
i fiammiferi	ee fyam**meefairee**	matches
la fibbia	la **feeb**bya	buckle
il fienile	eel fye**neelay**	hay loft
il fieno	eel **fye**no	hay
la figlia	la **fee**lya	daughter
il figlio	eel **fee**lyo	son
la finestra	la fee**nestra**	window
i fiori	ee **fyo**ree	flowers
il fischietto	eel fees**kyetto**	whistle
il fiume	eel **fyoo**may	river
il flauto dolce	eel **flowto dolchay**	recorder
la foca	la **foka**	seal
le foglie	lay **folyay**	leaves

il football americano	eel **foot**bol amaireee**kano**	American football
le forbici	lay **for**beechee	scissors
le forchette	lay for**kettay**	forks
il forcone	eel for**konay**	garden fork
la foresta	la fo**resta**	forest
il formaggio	eel for**majjo**	cheese
le forme	lay **formay**	shapes
il fornaio	eel forna-yo	baker (man)
la fornaia	la forna-ya	baker (woman)
la foschia	la **foskya**	mist
le fotografie	lay fotografee-ay	photos
il fotografo	eel fo**tografo**	photographer
la fragola	la **fragola**	strawberry
il fratello	eel fra**tello**	brother
le frecce	lay **frechay**	arrows
freddo	**freddo**	cold
il frigorifero	eel freego**reefairo**	fridge
la frittata	la freet**tata**	omelette
le frittelle	lay freet**tellay**	pancakes
la frutta	la **frootta**	fruit
il frutteto	eel frut**tayto**	orchard
il fucile	eel foo**cheelay**	gun
il fumetto	eel foo**metto**	comic
il fumo	eel **foomo**	smoke
il funambolo	eel foo**nambolo**	tightrope walker
la fune	la **foonay**	rope
il fungo	eel **foongo**	mushroom
i fuochi d'artificio	ee **fwo**kee darteee**feecho**	fireworks
fuori	**fwo**ree	outside
il furgone	eel foor**gonay**	van

G

la gabbia	la **gabbya**	cage
il gabbiano	eel gabb**yano**	seagull
la galleria	la gallai**reea**	tunnel
le galline	lay gal**leenay**	hens
il gallo	eel **gallo**	cockerel
la gamba	la **gamba**	leg
il gattino	eel gatt**eeno**	kitten
il gatto	eel **gatto**	cat
il gelato	eel je**lato**	ice cream
i gessetti	ee jes**settee**	chalks
il gesso	eel **jesso**	plaster
il giallo	eel **jallo**	yellow
il giardino	eel jar**deeno**	garden
la ginnastica artistica	la jeenn**asteeka** ar**teesteeka**	gymnastics
il ginocchio	eel jeenokk**yo**	knee
giocare	jo**karay**	to play
i giocattoli	ee jo**kattolee**	toys
il giocoliere	eel joko**lyairay**	juggler
il giornale	eel jor**nalay**	newspaper
i giorni	ee **jor**nee	days
i giorni speciali	ee **jor**nee spech**alee**	special days
la giostra	la **jostra**	merry-go-round
giovedì	jove**dee**	Thursday
la giraffa	la jee**raffa**	giraffe
i girini	ee jee**reenee**	tadpoles
giù	**joo**	down
il giubbotto	eel joobb**otto**	jacket
il giudice	eel **joo**deechay	judge
il gomito	eel **gomeeto**	elbow
la gomma	la **gomma**	rubber
la gonna	la **gonna**	skirt
il gorilla	eel go**reella**	gorilla

il granchio	*eel gran*kyo	crab
grande	*gran*day	big
grasso	*gras*so	fat
il grembiule	eel grem*byoo*lay	apron
il grigio	eel *gree*jo	grey
la gru	*la groo*	crane
le grucce	lay *groo*chay	crutches
la guancia	*la gwan*cha	cheek
il guanciale	eel gwan*cha*lay	pillow
i guanti	ee *gwan*tee	gloves
guardare	gwar*dar*ay	to look
il guinzaglio	eel gween*tsal*yo	lead
il gufo	eel *goo*fo	owl

H

l'hamburger (m)	*lam*boorgair	hamburger
l'hostess (f)	*lost*ess	air hostess

I

l'iceberg (m)	*lies*bairg	iceberg
l'imbianchino (m)	leembyan*kee*no	house painter
in cima	een *chee*ma	on top
in fondo	een *fon*do	at the bottom
l'infermiere (m)	leenfair*myair*ay	nurse (man)
l'infermiera (f)	leenfair*myair*a	nurse (woman)
l'ingresso (m)	leen*gres*so	hall
l'insalata (f)	leensa*la*ta	salad
l'insegnante (m/f)	leensen*yan*tay	teacher
l'interruttore (m)	leentairroot*tor*ay	switch
l'inverno (m)	leen*vair*no	winter
l'ippopotamo (m)	leeppo*po*tamo	hippopotamus
l'isola (f)	*lee*zola	island

J

i jeans	ee jeens	jeans
il jogging	eel *jog*geeng	jogging
il judo	eel *joo*do	judo

K

il karatè	eel kara*tay*	karate
il ketchup	eel *ke*chap	ketchup

L

le labbra	lay *lab*bra	lips
il laboratorio	eel labora*tor*yo	workshop
i lacci per le scarpe	ee *la*chee pair lay *skar*pay	shoelaces
il lago	eel *la*go	lake
la lampada	la *lam*pada	lamp
la lampadina	la lampa*dee*na	light bulb
il lampione	eel lamp*yon*ay	street lamp
il lampo	eel *lam*po	lightning

il lampone	eel lamp*on*ay	raspberry
lanciare	lan*char*ay	to throw
il latte	eel *lat*tay	milk
la lattuga	la lat*too*ga	lettuce
la lavagna	la la*van*ya	board
il lavandino	eel lavan*dee*no	basin
lavarsi	la*var*see	to wash
la lavatrice	la lava*tree*chay	washing machine
il lavello	eel la*vel*lo	sink
lavorare a maglia	lavor*ar*ay a *mal*ya	to knit
leggere	*lej*jairay	to read
il legno	eel *len*yo	wood
lento	*len*to	slow
il lenzuolo	eel lent*swo*lo	sheet
i leoncini	ee layon*chee*nee	lion cubs
il leone	eel lay*on*ay	lion
il leopardo	eel layo*par*do	leopard
le lettere	lay *let*tairay	letters
il letto	eel *let*to	bed
i libri	ee *lee*bree	books
la lima	la *lee*ma	file
il limone	eel lee*mon*ay	lemon
la lingua	la *leen*gwa	tongue
il locomotore	eel lokomo*tor*ay	engine (train)
lontano	lon*tan*o	far
la lucertola	la loo*chair*tola	lizard
la luna	la *loo*na	moon
il luna park	eel *loo*na park	funfair
lunedì	loonay*dee*	Monday
lungo	*loon*go	long
il lupo	eel *loo*po	wolf

M

la macchina	la *ma*keena	car
la macchina da corsa	la *ma*keena da *kor*sa	racing car
la macchina della polizia	la *ma*keena *del*la poleet*see*a	police car
la macchina fotografica	la *ma*keena fota*gra*feeka	camera
il macchinista	eel makkee*nees*ta	train driver
il macellaio	eel ma*chel*la-yo	butcher
la madre	la *ma*dray	mother
la maglietta	la mal*yet*ta	tee-shirt
il maglione	eel mal*yon*ay	pull-over
magro	*ma*gro	thin
i maiali	ee ma-*ya*lee	pigs
i maialini	ee ma-ya*lee*nee	piglets
il mandarino	eel manda*ree*no	clementine
mangiare	man*jar*ay	to eat
la maniglia della porta	la ma*nee*lya *del*la *por*ta	door handle
la mano	la *ma*no	hand
il mappamondo	eel mappa*mon*do	globe
il marciapiede	eel marcha*pye*day	pavement
il mare	eel *mar*ay	sea
il marinaio	eel maree*na*-yo	sailor
le marionette	lay maryo*net*tay	puppets
il marito	eel ma*ree*to	husband
la marmellata	la marmel*la*ta	jam
il marrone	eel mar*ron*ay	brown
martedì	marte*dee*	Tuesday
il martello	eel mar*tel*lo	hammer
il martello pneumatico	eel mar*tel*lo pnayooma*tee*ko	pneumatic drill
le maschere	lay *mas*kairay	masks
i massi	ee *mas*see	rocks

60

la matita	*la mateeta*	pencil
il matrimonio	*eel matreemonyo*	wedding
la mattina	*la matteena*	morning
le mattonelle	*lay mattonellay*	tiles
i mattoni	*ee mattonee*	bricks
la mazza	*la mattsa*	bat (sports)
me stesso	*may stesso*	myself
i meccanici	*ee mekkaneechee*	mechanics
la medicina	*la medeecheena*	medicine
la mela	*la mayla*	apple
il melone	*eel maylonay*	melon
il mento	*eel mento*	chin
il mercato	*eel mairkato*	market
mercoledi	*mairkolaydee*	Wednesday
i mestieri	*ee mestyairee*	jobs
i mestoli	*ee mestolee*	wooden spoons
il metro	*eel metro*	tape measure
il miele	*eel myelay*	honey
la minestra	*la meenestra*	soup
la moglie	*la molyay*	wife
molti	*moltee*	many
la mongolfiera	*la mongolfyaira*	hot air balloon
la montagna	*la montanya*	mountain
le montagne russe	*lay montanyay roossay*	rollercoaster
la moquette	*la mokett*	fitted carpet
morbido	*morbeedo*	soft
la morsa	*la morsa*	vice
morto	*morto*	dead
la mosca	*la moska*	fly
la motocicletta	*la motocheekletta*	motorbike
il motore	*eel motoray*	engine (car)
il motoscafo	*eel motoskafo*	motor boat
la mucca	*la mookka*	cow
il mucchio di fieno	*eel mookkyo dee fyeno*	haystack
il mulino a vento	*eel mooleeno a vento*	windmill
la musicassetta	*la moozeekassetta*	cassette
le mutande	*lay mootanday*	underpants

N

nascondersi	*naskondairsee*	to hide
il naso	*eel nazo*	nose
il nastro	*eel nastro*	ribbon
Natale	*natalay*	Christmas
la nave	*la navay*	ship
la nebbia	*la nebbya*	fog
il negozio	*eel negotsyo*	shop
il nero	*eel nairo*	black
la neve	*la nayvay*	snow
il nido	*eel needo*	nest
la nonna	*la nonna*	grandmother
il nonno	*eel nonno*	grandfather
la notte	*la nottay*	night
nove	*novay*	nine
i numeri	*ee noomairee*	numbers
il nuoto	*eel nwoto*	swimming
nuovo	*nwovo*	new
le nuvole	*lay noovolay*	clouds

O

l'occhio (m)	*lokkyo*	eye
le oche	*lay okay*	geese
l'olio (m)	*lolyo*	oil
l'ombrello (m)	*lombrello*	umbrella
l'ombrellone (m)	*lombrellonay*	beach umbrella

le onde	*lay onday*	waves
l'orchestra (f)	*lorkestra*	orchestra
le orecchie	*lay orekkyay*	ears
l'orologio (m)	*lorolojo*	clock, watch
l'orsacchiotto (m)	*lorsakkyotto*	teddy bear
l'orso (m)	*lorso*	bear
l'orso (m) polare	*lorso polaray*	polar bear
l'ospedale (m)	*lospedalay*	hospital
l'osso (m)	*losso*	bone
otto	*otto*	eight
l'ovale (m)	*lovalay*	oval

P

la padella	*la padella*	frying pan
il padre	*eel padray*	father
la pagaia	*la paga-ya*	paddle
il pagliaccio	*eel palyacho*	clown
il palazzo	*eel palattso*	block of flats, building
la paletta (da giardino)	*la paletta (da jardeeno)*	trowel
la paletta (da spiaggia)	*la paletta (da spyajja)*	beach spade
la paletta (per la spazzatura)	*la paletta (pair la spattsatoora)*	dustpan
la palla	*la palla*	ball
la pallacanestro	*la pallakanestro*	basketball
il palloncino	*eel palloncheeno*	balloon
la panchina	*la pankeena*	bench
la pancia	*la pancha*	tummy
il panda	*eel panda*	panda
il pane	*eel panay*	bread
il pane tostato	*eel panay tostato*	toast
il panino	*eel paneeno*	sandwich
la panna	*la panna*	cream
il pannolino	*eel pannoleeno*	nappy
i pantaloncini	*ee pantaloncheenee*	shorts
i pantaloni	*ee pantalonee*	trousers
le pantofole	*lay pantofolay*	slippers
il pappagallino	*eel pappagalleeno*	budgerigar
il pappagallo	*eel pappagallo*	parrot
il paracadute	*eel parakadootay*	parachute
il parco	*eel parko*	park
la parete	*la paraytay*	wall
parlare	*parlaray*	to talk
il parrucchiere	*eel parrookkyairay*	hairdresser
il passeggino	*eel passejjeeno*	pushchair
i pastelli	*ee pastellee*	crayons
i pasti	*ee pastee*	meals
la pastorella	*la pastorella*	shepherdess
le patate	*lay patatay*	potatoes
le patatine	*lay patateenay*	crisps
le patatine fritte	*lay patateenay freettay*	chips
il pattinaggio su ghiaccio	*eel patteenajjio soo gyacho*	ice skating
i pattini	*ee patteenee*	skates
la pattumiera	*la pattoomyaira*	rubbish bin
il pavimento	*eel paveemento*	floor
le pecore	*lay paykoray*	sheep
il pellicano	*eel pelleekano*	pelican
la penna	*la penna*	pen
i pennarelli	*ee pennarellee*	felt-tips
il pennello	*eel pennello*	paintbrush
pensare	*pensaray*	to think
la pensilina	*la penseeleena*	platform
le pentole	*le pentolay*	pans

61

il pepe	eel *pay*pay	pepper
la pera	la *pai*ra	pear
le perline	lay pair*lee*nay	beads
la pesca (frutto)	la *pes*ka (*froo*tto)	peach
la pesca (attività)	la *pes*ka (atte*vee*ta)	fishing
il pescatore	eel peska*tor*ay	fisherman
il pesce	eel *pe*shay	fish
il peschereccio	eel peskai*re*cho	fishing boat
i pesci rossi	ee *pe*shee *ros*see	goldfish
la petroliera	la petrol*yai*ra	oil tanker
il pettine	eel *pet*teenay	comb
la pialla	la *pyal*la	plane (shaving)
il pianeta	eel pya*nay*ta	planet
piangere	*pyan*jairay	to cry
il piano di lavoro	eel *pya*no dee *lavo*ro	workbench
il pianoforte	eel pyano*for*tay	piano
la pianta	la *pyan*ta	plant
i piatti	ee *pyat*tee	plates
i piattini	ee pyat*tee*nee	saucers
il piccione	eel *pee*chonay	pigeon
piccolo	*peek*kolo	small
il picnic	eel *peek*neek	picnic
il piede	eel *pye*day	foot
pieno	*pye*no	full
le pietre	lay *pye*tray	stones
il pigiama	eel *pee*jama	pyjamas
le pillole	lay *peel*lolay	pills
il pilota	eel *pee*lota	pilot
il ping-pong	eel *peeng*-pong	ping-pong
il pinguino	eel peeng*wee*no	penguin
le pinne	lay *peen*nay	flippers
la pioggia	la *pyoj*ja	rain
il pipistrello	eel peepees*trel*lo	bat (animal)
la piscina	la pee*shee*na	swimming pool
i piselli	ee pee*zel*lee	peas
la pista di atterraggio	la *pees*ta dee attair*raj*jo	runway
le piume	lay *pyoo*may	feathers
il piumone	eel pyoo*mo*nay	duvet
la pizza	la *peet*sa	pizza
la plastilina	la plastee*lee*na	modelling dough
il pneumatico	lo pnayoo*mateeko	tyre
pochi	*po*kee	few
i poliziotti	ee poleet*syot*tee	policemen
il pollaio	eel *pol*la-yo	hen-house
il pollice	eel *pol*leechay	thumb
il pollo	eel *pol*lo	chicken
il pomodoro	eel pomo*do*ro	tomato
il pompelmo	eel pom*pel*mo	grapefruit
il pompiere	eel pom*pyai*ray	fireman
il ponte	eel *pon*tay	bridge
il pony	eel *po*nee	pony
il pop-corn	eel *pop*-korn	popcorn
il porcellino d'India	eel porchel*lee*no *deen*dya	guinea pig
il porcile	eel porch*ee*lay	pigsty
il porro	eel *por*ro	leek
la porta	la *por*ta	door
il portabagagli	eel portaba*gal*yee	boot (of car)
portare	por*tar*ay	to carry
i poster	ee *pos*tair	posters
il postino	eel pos*tee*no	postman
la pozzanghera	eel pott*san*gaira	puddle
il pranzo	eel *pran*tso	lunch, dinner
prendere	*pren*dairay	to take
la primavera	la preema*vai*ra	spring
primo	*pree*mo	first
la proboscide	la probo*shee*day	trunk
il prosciutto	eel pro*shoot*to	ham
i pulcini	ee pool*chee*nee	chickens
pulito	poo*lee*to	clean
le puntine da disegno	lay poon*tee*nay da dee*se*nyo	drawing pins
il purè	eel poo*ray	mashed potato
il puzzle	eel *pa*zol	puzzle

Q

il quaderno	eel kwa*dair*no	notebook
il quadrato	eel kwa*dra*to	square
quattordici	kwat*tor*deechee	fourteen
quattro	*kwat*tro	four
quindici	*kween*deechee	fifteen

R

la racchetta	la rak*ket*ta	racquet
raccogliere	rak*kol*yairay	to pick
il radiatore	eel radya*tor*ay	radiator
la radio	la *rad*yo	radio
la ragnatela	la ranya*tay*la	spider's web
il ragno	eel *ran*yo	spider
i ramoscelli	ee ramo*shel*lee	twigs
la rana	la *ra*na	frog
il rastrello	eel ras*trel*lo	rake
il razzo	eel *rat*tso	rocket
il regalo	eel re*ga*lo	present
il remo	eel *re*mo	oar
la renna	la *ren*na	reindeer
i respingenti	ee respeen*jen*tee	buffers
la rete	la *ray*tay	net
la rete di sicurezza	la *ray*tay dee seekoo*ret*tsa	safety net
il rettangolo	eel ret*tan*golo	rectangle
il riccio	eel *ree*cho	hedgehog
ridere	*ree*dairay	to laugh
il righello	eel ree*gel*lo	ruler
il rimorchio	eel reemor*kyo	trailer
il rinoceronte	eel reenochai*ron*tay	rhinoceros
il riso	eel *re*zo	rice
il robot	eel *ro*bot	robot
i rollerblades	ee *roller*blades	rollerblades
il rombo	eel *rom*bo	diamond (shape)
rompere	*rom*pairay	to break
il rosa	eel *ro*za	pink
il rospo	eel *ros*po	toad
il rosso	eel *ros*so	red
la roulotte	la roo*lott*	caravan
il rubinetto	eel roobee*net*to	tap
il rugby	eel *rag*bee	rugby
la rugiada	la roo*ja*da	dew
la ruota	la *rwo*ta	wheel, big wheel
il ruscello	eel roo*shel*lo	stream

S

sabato	*sa*bato	Saturday
la sala d'aspetto	la *sa*la das*pet*to	waiting room
il salame	eel sa*la*may	salami
il sale	eel *sa*lay	salt
la salsiccia	la sal*see*cha	sausage
saltare	sal*tar*ay	to jump
saltare la corda	sal*tar*ay la *kor*da	to skip
il salvadanaio	eel salva*da*na-yo	money box

i sandali	ee **sandal**ee	sandals
il sapone	eel sapo**nay**	soap
la scala	la **ska**la	ladder
la scala di corda	la **ska**la dee **kor**da	rope ladder
le scale	lay **ska**lay	stairs
gli scalini	lyee skal**ee**nee	steps
le scarpe	lay **skar**pay	shoes
le scarpe da ginnastica	lay **skar**pay da jeen**nas**teeka	trainers
la scatola	la **ska**tola	box
scavare	ska**va**ray	to dig
la scavatrice	la skava**tree**chay	bulldozer
lo schiacciasassi	lo skyacha**sas**see	roller
la schiena	la **sky**ena	back
gli sci	lyee shee	skis
lo sci	lo shee	skiing
lo sci nautico	lo shee **now**teeko	waterskiing
la sciarpa	la **shar**pa	scarf
la scimmia	la **sheem**mya	monkey
lo scivolo	lo **shee**volo	slide, helter-skelter
le scodelle	lay sko**del**lay	bowls
la scogliera	la skol**yair**a	cliff
lo scoiattolo	lo skoy**at**tolo	squirrel
la scopa	la **sko**pa	broom
scrivere	**skree**vairay	to write
la scuderia	la skoodai**ree**a	stable
la scuola	la **skwo**la	school
scuro	**skoo**ro	dark
il secchiello	eel sek**kyel**lo	bucket
il sedano	eel **se**dano	celery
il sedere	eel se**dair**ay	bottom
la sedia	la **se**dya	chair
la sedia a rotelle	la **se**dya a ro**tel**lay	wheelchair
la sedia a sdraio	la **se**dya a **zdra**-yo	deckchair
sedici	**say**deechee	sixteen
la sega	la **say**ga	saw
la segatura	la sayga**toor**a	sawdust
la seggiovia	la seijo**vee**a	chairlift
i segnali	ee sen**ya**lee	signals
sei	say	six
la sella	la **sel**la	saddle
il semaforo	eel se**ma**foro	traffic lights
i semi	ee **say**mee	seeds
il sentiero	eel sen**tyai**ro	path
la sera	la **sai**ra	evening
il serpente	eel sair**pen**tay	snake
la serra	la **sair**ra	greenhouse
sette	**set**tay	seven
lo sgabello	lo zga**bel**lo	stool
la siepe	la **sye**pay	hedge
sinistra	see**nees**tra	left
la siringa	la see**reen**ga	syringe
lo skateboard	lo **sket**bord	skateboard
la slitta	la **sleet**ta	sleigh
lo snowboard	lo **sno**bord	snowboard
soffiare	soffi**ya**ray	to blow
il soffitto	eel sof**feet**to	ceiling
il soggiorno	eel soj**jor**no	living room
i soldatini	ee solda**tee**nee	toy soldiers
i soldi	ee **sol**dee	money
il sole	eel **so**lay	sun
sopra	**so**pra	above
le sopracciglia	lay sopra**cheel**ya	eyebrows
la sorella	la sor**el**la	sister
sorridere	sor**ree**dairay	to smile
sotto	**sot**to	below
il sottomarino	eel sottoma**ree**no	submarine
spaccare	spak**ka**ray	to chop
gli spaghetti	lyee spa**get**tee	spaghetti
lo spago	lo **spa**go	string
le spalle	lay **spal**lay	shoulders
lo spaventapasseri	lo spaventa**pas**sairee	scarecrow
lo Spazio	lo **spat**syo	space
spazzare	spatt**sa**ray	to sweep
la spazzatura	la spatt**sa**toora	rubbish
la spazzola	la **spatt**sola	brush, hairbrush
lo spazzolino	lo spatt**sol**eeno	toothbrush
lo spazzolone	lo spatt**sol**onay	mop
lo specchio	lo **spek**kyo	mirror
la spiaggia	la **spy**ajja	beach
la spilla	la **speel**la	badge
gli spinaci	lyee spee**na**chee	spinach
spingere	**speen**jairay	to push
lo spogliatoio	lo spolya**toy**o	changing room
sporco	**spor**ko	dirty
lo sport	lo sport	sport
la sposa	la **spo**za	bride
lo sposo	lo **spo**zo	bridegroom
la spugna	la **spoon**ya	sponge
lo squalo	lo **skwa**lo	shark
la staccionata	la stacho**na**ta	fence
le stagioni	lay sta**jo**nee	seasons
lo stagno	lo **stan**yo	pond
la stalla	la **stal**la	cowshed
stare seduti	**sta**ray sedo**tee**	to sit
la stazione di servizio	la **stat**syonay dee sair**veet**syo	garage
la stazione ferroviaria	la **stat**syonay fairro**vyar**ya	station
la stella	la **stel**la	star
la stella marina	la **stel**la mar**ee**na	starfish
lo steward	lo **styoo**ward	air steward
gli stivali di gomma	lyee steeva**lee** dee **gom**ma	boots, wellies
lo straccio	lo **stra**cho	duster
la strada	la **stra**da	street
le strisce pedonali	lay **stree**shay pedo**na**lee	pedestrian crossing
lo struzzo	lo **stroot**tso	ostrich
su	soo	up
il subacqueo	eel soo**bak**kwayo	diver
il succo di frutta	eel **sook**ko dee **froot**ta	fruit juice
il sumo	eel **soo**mo	sumo wrestling
la susina	la soo**zee**na	plum

T

i tacchini	ee tak**kee**nee	turkeys
tagliare	tal**ya**ray	to cut
la talpa	la **tal**pa	mole
i tamburi	ee tam**boo**ree	drums
il tappetino	eel tappay**tee**no	rug
il tappeto	eel tap**pay**to	carpet
la tartaruga	la tarta**roo**ga	tortoise
le tasche	lay **tas**kay	pockets
il tasso	eel **tas**so	badger
il tavolino	eel tavo**lee**no	small table
il taxi	eel **tak**see	taxi
le tazze	lay **tatt**say	cups
il tè	eel tay	tea
la teiera	la ta**yai**ra	teapot
il telefono	eel te**le**fono	telephone
il telescopio	eel teles**kop**yo	telescope
il televisore	eel televee**zor**ay	television
il temperino	eel tempe**ree**no	penknife
il tempo	eel **tem**po	weather
la tenda	la **ten**da	curtain, tent
le tende	lay **ten**day	curtains, tents

il tennis	eel **tennees**	tennis
il termometro	eel tairm**mo**maytro	thermometer
la terra	la **tairra**	earth
la testa	la **testa**	head
il tetto	eel **tetto**	roof
la tigre	la **teegray**	tiger
tirare	teer**aray**	to pull
il tiro a segno	eel **teero** a sen**yo**	rifle range
il tiro al cerchietto	eel **teero** al chair**kyetto**	hoop-la
il tiro con l'arco	eel **teero** kon **larko**	archery
il topolino	eel topo**leeno**	mouse
il torace	eel tora**chay**	chest
il toro	eel **toro**	bull
la torre di controllo	la **torray** dee kon**trollo**	control tower
la torta	la **torta**	cake, birthday cake
il tosaerba	eel toza-**airba**	lawnmower
la tovaglia	la to**valya**	tablecloth
il trapano	eel **trapano**	drill
il trapezio	eel tra**pet**syo	trapeze
i trasporti	ee tra**sportee**	transport
il trattore	eel trat**toray**	tractor
tre	tray	three
tredici	**tray**deechee	thirteen
il trenino	eel tray**neeno**	toy train
il trenino dei fantasmi	eel tray**neeno** day fant**az**mee	ghost train
il treno	eel **trayno**	train
il treno merci	eel **trayno** mairchee	goods train
il triangolo	eel tree**angolo**	triangle
il triciclo	eel tree**cheeklo**	tricycle
la tromba	la **tromba**	trumpet
i trucioli	ee **trooch**yolee	shavings
il tubo di gomma	eel **toobo** dee **gomma**	hosepipe
i tuffi	ee **tooffee**	diving

U

gli uccelli	lyee ooch**ellee**	birds
ultimo	**oolteemo**	last
undici	**oondeechee**	eleven
uno	**oono**	one
l'uomo (m)	**lwomo**	man
le uova	lay **wova**	eggs
l'uovo (m) fritto	**lwovo freetto**	fried egg
l'uovo (m) sodo	**lwovo sodo**	hard-boiled egg
l'uva	**loova**	grapes

V

la vacanza	la va**kantsa**	holiday
i vagoni	ee va**gonee**	carriages
la valigia	la va**leeja**	suitcase
la vanga	la **vanga**	spade
la vasca	la **vaska**	bath
il vassoio	eel vas**soyo**	tray
vecchio	**vekkyo**	old
la vela	la **vayla**	sailing
veloce	vay**lochay**	fast
venerdì	venair**dee**	Friday
venti	**ventee**	twenty
il vento	eel **vento**	wind
il verde	eel **vairday**	green
la verdura	la vair**doora**	vegetables
il verme	eel **vairmay**	worm
la vernice	la vairnee**chay**	paint
la vespa	la **vespa**	wasp

la vestaglia	la ves**talya**	dressing gown
i vestiti	ee ves**teetee**	clothes
il vestito	eel ves**teeto**	dress
il veterinario	eel vetairee**naryo**	vet
vicino	vee**cheeno**	near
la videocassetta	la veedayoka**ssetta**	video
il vigile urbano	eel **veejeelay** oor**bano**	policeman (traffic police)
il villaggio	eel veel**lajjo**	village
il viola	eel **vyola**	purple
il viso	eel **veezo**	face
il vitello	eel vee**tello**	calf
le viti	lay **veetee**	screws
vivo	**veevo**	alive
il volo libero	eel **volo leebairo**	hang gliding
i volpacchiotti	ee volpak**kyottee**	fox cubs
la volpe	la **volpay**	fox
vuoto	**vwoto**	empty

W

il water	eel **vatair**	toilet
il windsurf	eel **weensairf**	windsurfing

Y

lo yogurt	lo **yo**goort	yoghurt

Z

lo zaino	lo **tsa**-eeno	backpack
le zampe	lay **tsam**pay	paws
la zappa	lu **tsappa**	hoe
la zebra	la **tsebra**	zebra
la zia	la **tseea**	aunt
lo zio	lo **tseeo**	uncle
lo zoo	lo tsoo	zoo
la zucca	la **tsookka**	pumpkin
lo zucchero	lo **tsookk**airo	sugar
lo zucchero filato	lo **tsookk**airo fee**lato**	candy floss

This revised edition first published in 1999 by Usborne Publishing Ltd, Usborne House, 83-85 Saffron Hill, London EC1N 8RT, England.
www.usborne.com
Based on a previous title first published in 1983.